Let's Be Realistic: Battling Epilepsy and Other Limitations

By Darnelle Beckford

First Edition: June 2021

Let's Be Realistic: Battling Epilepsy and Other Limitations/ By Darnelle Beckford

ISBN: 978-1-943616-41-1

Publisher: MAWMedia Group, LLC
Los Angeles | Reno | Nashville

Acknowledgements

The people I really want to thank have stood by me my whole life:
Mom, Dad, Sister, Brother. To mom and dad, you two did the
grunt work. You asked the tough questions about epilepsy and
challenged the system to get better to support me. **Mom**, you
worked 16 hours a day, left work running on fumes, and drove me
around to special appointments. You secured my drive. In the words
of Tupac, "I can't thank you enough for the sweet things you've done
for me." I know you have my back no matter what. I know my
condition stressed you out and even resulted in weight loss. I want to
simply say, Thank You! I hope I made you proud by beating the odds.
I hope you are happy with where I have reached, the path I
consistently walk, and your contribution in raising a Black man today.
Dad, you are one of the reasons I am so levelheaded. My personality
is a mix of mom and dad, AND my advice seeking is sponsored by
you. You put me in sports activities and other positive groups.

Because of you, I have a vision of managing friends, family, and businesses, never mixing their values as separate benefits. You taught me to put family first and maintain boundaries, never putting the fickle, vanity needs of others ahead of my own health and wellbeing. **Patrese**, you are a combination of sister and best friend. You were present through my struggles and my triumphs. You helped me realize that I could do anything, showing me an example of grit, ingenuity, and strength, directly and indirectly. I always want to be around you because you are an extension of our mother. You will forever be the other ear and my advocate. I have learned to enjoy the little and the big things from you. There is nothing I can do to pay you back for all the attention my illness commanded. I envied the attention you received—the attention of being "normal." You taught me never to settle. You taught me that good enough is never good enough. I learned to fight from you. I love you. I am always here for you no matter what. **Patrick Saint Anthony**, my brother, even though we did not see each other much in our younger years, my preteens and adulthood have been influenced by you. No matter how many challenges you have faced, you continue to climb. You are the smartest of us. I learned perseverance and autonomy from you because you never allowed mistakes to define you. I will always be in your corner. Whether we text for 5 minutes or talk for an hour, we connect in a way only brothers can.

To all my extended family and friends, I love you. Thank you for being there for the little things and the big things. For both sides of my family, you were there. You taught me life lessons. You showed me how to maneuver, what to look out for, and how to carry myself. All others I could not name, thank you for being a part of my life.

Dr. Jayoung Pak was my first neurologist at UMDNJ. I was her first patient. She treated me like her own son. Vegas nerve stimulation was her success. There is no limit my family and I would not cross for you. Thank you to you and your staff.

THANK YOU TO AND FOR

By Darnelle Beckford

Inspired by the song "Pressure" from Vybz Kartel and Teejay, and "Not an Easy Road" from Buju Baton

Thank you to the struggle and also for seeing the bigger picture

Thank you to the mentors that came along the way for showing me different ways to learn

Thank you to the system for waking up a giant in me and for setting the bar low

Thank you to my family on the Manchester and on the Trelawny side for the memories and life lessons

Thank you to my mommy, daddy, sister, and brother for giving me the tools to win, for knocking down doors, for sacrifice and sleepless nights

Thank you to the doctor that told my parents I wouldn't be anything

Thank you to dancehall, and reggae music for painting pictures on not giving up and many more messages

Thank you to my seizures for coming into my life to unlock the potential and beast in me and for putting that chip on my shoulder

And finally, thank you for the sayings, wanti wanti can't get it, getti getti no wanti (have nots covet what the haves take for granted). Nuh listen to di noise, watch di sale (do not be misled by others excitement; use the facts to judge for yourself).

Table of Contents

Let's Be Realistic

Intelligence is the capacity to receive, decode, and transmit information efficiently. Stupidity is blockage of this process at any point. Bigotry, ideologies, etc. block the ability to receive; robotic reality—tunnels—block the ability to decode or integrate new signals; censorship blocks transmission.

ROBERT ANTON WILSON

Darnelle Beckford

Preface by Darnelle

Living with a disability is an everyday struggle for most; no matter the type of disability. This book is all about inspiring people who have gone through or are currently going through struggles. This book is not another stale narrative about a Black family in decline or the ravages of drugs, alcohol, and broken families. After reading this book, you will know things about me that some will find heroic, wondering how I got through life's challenges. I endured more than most, but with positive support from loved ones, I was able to make it through any obstacle.

As someone living with a disability, I deal with certain things internally that some people do not realize. Sometimes, I deal with depression and even low self-esteem. The purpose of this book is not only to share my story of living with seizures and how I overcame living with a disability, but it is simply to motivate, inspire and empower

Let's Be Realistic

those who are dealing with their own struggles. This book is intended to reassure people that regardless of their struggles or disabilities, they can still reach their God-given potential in life.

It took me a long time to learn, but my comprehension came with time. I know it is frustrating when a parent or teacher must remind themselves to be patient with a student. At the same time, we must adopt a new narrative. The disadvantages of a child do not define them. AND I had to work my butt off for what I have achieved. This work ethic is a requirement. A supportive environment constructs the ladder for those like me to climb. It provides the tools, raw materials, and instructions. I will build the ladder myself if I must. I wrote my story as a guide for others to be inspired to take up tools, find materials, research instructions, and build their own ladders.

What I Learned. Each chapter presents WHAT I LEARNED. I want you to know what I learned, the emotion of the lessons, and the elements that I took from my experiences. I wished all my teachers would have engaged beyond the lesson. Some did, and I appreciated that. Having a chance to walk in their shoes before attempting comprehension or skill application was encouraging. It took away some of the fear as I saw that they did not always get it on the first try. I could try and try again just as they did.

Darnelle Beckford

Application to You. Another addition to each chapter is the APPLICATION TO YOU message. I am convinced that setting up what you may get from my experience creates an opportunity for discussion. It fits with one of the central points of the book: ask questions. The dialogue, whether you agree or disagree, expand or expunge, flow or resist my application or suggestions. We can talk. We can challenge each other in the process. My thick skin, having been broken and counted out uniquely, has prepared me for these discussions. I also know that these discussions will enhance both comprehension and learning.

I offered my Mom and Dad an opportunity to provide forewords for my book. I also wanted to present gratitude to my siblings. Without the support of my family, including my sister and brother, I would not have achieved what I achieved. I would honestly not be alive if my sister was not looking out for me. My siblings still look out for me to this day. There is nothing I would not do for them. Without them, I would not be the person I am. I would be completely different with regards to trust and life experience.

My parents have been a blessing as well. I am happy to always surpass their expectations and reset their bar for me to a higher level. I appreciate what my parents did for me. They provided the perfect balance of 1) caution and worry that I could not achieve and 2) support

Let's Be Realistic

and experiences that challenged my limits. I can imagine that other parents do not get that balance right. My mom would work 16 hours per day, then turn around and get me to the neurologist on Saturdays. My dad would involve me in baseball and other community activities. My extended family also seemed to make sacrifices and contribute intentionally to my development.

Some people grow up with a chip on their shoulder because of their family. I grew up with support in my corner. My family gave me a vision of a better life. My parents did not know what to expect, but they encouraged me to strive. As my achievements grew, they were consistent. That balance challenged me to do more. I cannot thank them enough. I am proud with exceeding gratitude to present this book as another testament to the power of family and the power of leveraging their support to believe in oneself.

Darnelle Beckford

Mom's Reflections on the Story

As a Mom, I am much more engaged with the day-to-day. I do not worry about the philosophical reasoning and the political implications. I just want what is best for my son. The book provides a narrative that families and professionals can learn from. I am emotional when it comes to Darnelle. If I were to read his book, I may not be able to get through it. He overcame a great deal and achieved with admirable perseverance. I must gain the courage to get there.

Never Give Up

I encourage parents never to give up on their children. They will surprise you. To see how far Darnelle has come is surprising. It has been a long journey. He is very thoughtful. He has a good heart. He is the one who will check in on me, always there engaging to offer a drink or something to eat. He will do great things. I keep telling him, "You

Let's Be Realistic

may have epilepsy, but epilepsy does not have you. Work with it. Wherever you are, never be ashamed to say what it is. Those around you will be the ones to help you. Everyone has their own story. Never be ashamed to tell yours."

There is not much difference in the parenting experience between my daughter and Darnelle. My daughter was five when she found Darnelle during his first seizure. Sometimes, she thinks we put a great deal of (too much) attention on what Darnelle is doing. But she looks out for him too. She does not say anything, but I suspect she has those feelings. She should know that we love her and celebrate her. We also appreciate the sister she is to her brother.

The Power of a Village

The extended family is the most important part of the story. It was outside of the blood relations. The house we purchased came because of our acquaintance and supports. I can depend on people who are within walking distance to check in on us and Darnelle.

Darnelle knows that he has mommy when he needs me. He does not use it a lot because he wants to be independent. I think knowing that I am there allows him to be independent. I remember having to take him to school for a few days while he was in community college.

Darnelle Beckford

I joked with him that the degree was partially mine because of the time I sat in the parking lot waiting for him to finish a class.

When he finished elementary school, I was so proud. I could not believe that we had come that far. I remember that a neurologist came to us once when he was in the hospital early on. The doctor voiced that he was not sure that he would be able to perform beyond the simple usage of his hands. I am overjoyed and pinch myself that he has come from that moment to excelling. He continues to excel at every stage of the journey. He finished elementary. He finished high school. He finished community college as well. He had so many obstacles but has made unbelievable progress.

Learning as a Parent

Sometimes I think my history as a teacher informs my parenting. Most times I do not. Dealing with your own children is a different thought process than working with other people's children. In the beginning, we were just looking for answers. We wanted relief and some help. We took the doctor's judgment and went with it. We quickly learned the hard way to research more for ourselves. I double-checked medications and side effects. We had to limit his time with others or keep him with people who understood his diagnosis. It is still challenging for me. Darnelle and I talk about it often. As a mom, you

Let's Be Realistic

want to make sure he is going to be fine. I worry a lot. I am working to get better as he gets older. I want to trust that he understands what is going on and can fend for himself. I want to take him everywhere I go, but he has gained his own independence. I think I am being slightly selfish. I am not okay with it. I do not know how I will get rid of it. It is something I must work on. It is there. I cannot help it.

Darnelle Beckford

Dad's Reflections on the Story

As a Father, I see the book as a way of providing various perspectives on how health in America can impact a family. A supportive family is critical to the opportunity, development, and addressing of health needs. The contribution of the village or extended family (including strangers) is important. The other critical components are systems including the health care system and the educational system. The stereotypical reaction to neurological health issues can be a challenge to overcome. Institutions and professionals typically operate according to formulas. My suggestion is to look at each child as unique and deserving of specific, individualized care. Personally, I became more civically involved. Advocating for my son pushed me to do things that I would not have done ordinarily.

Let's Be Realistic

Our Love Story

My wife and I met in college in Jamaica. She was introduced to me while we were out with a group. Even though we were both otherwise attached, we shared an instant attraction. I migrated to the US. We corresponded through letters. Many people did not know that my wife and I met in a college that was specifically about training teachers. We had both been schoolteachers for a year or two prior to immigrating to the United States.

I was serving in the US Navy when our daughter was born in 1987. As my next tour of duty would be at sea, we decided it would be best to transition to reserve instead of being an absentee dad. Once my tour was up and I was discharged from active duty in 1989, we relocated to New Jersey where most of my family lived. Darnelle – a hyperactive, intelligent boy was added to the family in 1989.

We made a definitive choice of scheduling our work around our children. We firmly believed in the importance of having a caring home. We decided that we would provide this stable home by working alternate shifts. I would support the children during the day/evenings while my wife worked second shift.

Context on Schools

My son became ill for the first time while in a private Catholic school. They did not have the resources for special education. They

Darnelle Beckford

told us to go to public school. This was a source of fear for us. We have heard horror stories of the low-quality schools especially in urban areas where people of color lived. As former teachers, my wife and I both shared the view that school environments must be conducive for learning. I found out that the gray walls were by design. The system is created to get black children accustomed to the prison walls. I was involved in the community to some extent but never paid attention to the public school system. I had heard about Abbott v. Burke, the decision in 1985, but I was not actively involved.

I remember the first day. I walked up to the principal and introduced myself, wanting him to know that we were involved parents. I got an eerie feeling as I walked in. The walls were gray. I walked into the classroom and observed about 40 children under the care of one middle-aged, white woman. I was immediately uncomfortable. I had read about Emmitt Till. It is a common belief that white women learn to look at black males as prey. I knew that the environment was not conducive to learning.

The principal complained that they did not have money to do anything different. He suggested that I go to the school board meeting. He explained that there were opportunities to stand and ask questions. I remember the first meeting. I stood up in the line to

Let's Be Realistic

comment. "I don't understand why my school in Madison Avenue..."
They interrupted me.

"What agenda area are you talking about." I did not know that I
had to speak according to the agenda. I quickly looked at the posted
agenda and spoke up.

"I'm under the budget (as my request concerned a classroom aide
for his oversized class)" This was my first introduction to educational
advocacy.

About a month later, I put my hand in the air to be president of
the school PTA. A middle-aged woman voted for me to break the tie
between another woman and me. She told me later that my eagerness
was what convinced her. I went on to do a lot of advocacy work
throughout the community at multiple levels of influence. I was
involved with the Education Law Center focused on the plight of low-
income parents. They were stretched between their challenges of
wanting to show up for their children and providing for them
financially. I realized that parents were motivated when their children
receive awards.

I organized a benefit dinner with the keynote of a Citizenship
Award (this was later developed to be per marking period). I pitched
it to the mayor. She was quick to say that she could not pay for the

Darnelle Beckford

dinner. I appealed to local business owners, especially restaurants. I spoke practically about what could happen both positive and negative. I convinced them to supply food for me. The first event drew 300 people and politicians. I became good friends with the States' Education Commissioner. After months of emotional pleas at board meetings, I was able to leverage my new relationship with the Commissioner to get approval for all the classrooms. I also insisted that the students must have a say in choosing the colors.

As Department manager, I gained special allowance from my then-company President for an extended lunch 3 times weekly to be with Darnelle in his class as a "free personal aide." The complaint was that he was "disruptive" since we refused to fill prescriptions for the mood-altering drugs they were insisting upon.

Medications were a true challenge for us: I remember a few nights after Darnelle was discharged from a month-long hospital stay, I was preparing the dosage and muttered, "Darnelle, it's time for your Dilantin. Time for another seizure." *DAMN.* Slapping my hand to my forehead, I quickly opened my computer and looked up Dilantin. There, in BLACK & WHITE, were the side effects – "Seizure" I called UMDNJ Newark for the on-call neurologist who happened to be Dr. Kornishberg, Darnelle's personal neurologist. I angrily told Dr Kornishberg about the discovery I made. He told me he would call me back. He kept his promise within 3 minutes after hanging up with me. "Mr. Beckford," he empathized, "Don't give him that anymore. You can toss the Dilantin in the garbage and up the dose of the Depakote." Depakote's side effects included hyperactivity. The school wanted to put him on either Adderall or Ritalin to decrease his hyperactivity. Neurontin was another disaster. Sullenness and social withdrawal were the side effects of that medication. The lesson was for us to check each medication prescribed to our child. I counsel parents to always ask for help, question the doctors, and do their own research. Thank God for education, the Internet, and doctors who listen and partner with you in care.

The Progress and Achievement

Moving from Irvington to Somerset was a wake-up call. He was designated as hyperactive and special ed. It was depressing for him. As we moved into the new school district, my wife visited one school and returned bawling. She said, "It's like a mini prison."

He was recruited for a special education baseball team because of his status. But the coach noticed his athleticism and ability and challenged his disability status. He was then moved to the regular team. This example is central to my advocacy. Before that, no one had challenged him to be "normal." His only health challenge was seizures. He did not have other special education problems.

Darnelle Beckford

A consistent problem throughout his school years was that he was not being challenged in school. Around the time his older sister was preparing for college, I would take him along on college preview trips. He wanted to attend college. He was not sure what he wanted to do, but he voiced an interest in music production. We explored Full Sail University & Beacon College both in Orlando Florida and NY Arts School in Manhattan.

I finally asked him a question, "What do you get up in the morning thinking about without anyone saying anything to you?"

"I wake up thinking about cooking."

"Your talent is cooking. You can have the hobby of music producing."

"Okay. I will go to the community college and do food and beverage management."

The college we chose was supportive though there was still some stigma. He became more independent and self-assured while in the community college. He blossomed academically. I remember when we received the letter that he was on the Dean's List. He was receiving the same work. He was not being treated differently. He was met with the challenge, and he rose to the challenge.

Let's Be Realistic

The Good Part

Our village is our key to success. Over the years, our family and friends supported us throughout the process. My daughter and a close friend's daughter became good friends. They would keep the kids overnight when I would have school board duties. Our sister, who is a nurse, would provide us information on medications and dosages.

If it had not been for them, it would have been hard. My wife or I would have lost our jobs if we did not have that village. The lesson is that you cannot be isolated as a family. There are good people in the world.

Our church was another great support. I remember Pastor Seth attending one of my son's baseball games to see him play. The game was fantastic for him at shortstop and bat. They had children's groups where they included Darnelle. They were open to learning about his medication and how to engage most proactively with him.

The environment you surround your children with and how you engage with them creates the most lasting impression. My wife always says, "Oh yes, he's not the best husband, but he is the best father that our children can have." Giving our children the best of our ability, being their voices, advocating for their care and support is

Darnelle Beckford

crucial to their development. In addition to the physical support, the attention and example you provide as a parent is key.

The family and the village created what Darnelle is today. In addition, the process we endured through learning, advocacy, and seeking healing for him has made me a better person. I did not always learn the lessons right away, but I learned. It has driven me to different places. It has humbled me. I have been pushed to serve. I am grateful to have learned how to be a servant.

Section I: The Diagnosis

Darnelle Beckford

THE FOUNDATION
A Poem by Darnelle Beckford
Inspired by "Look into my Eyes"
from Bounty Killer

The foundation is built to last for years even for generations

The foundation is those who are willing to create and who are going to fight

The foundation is unbreakable, firm, and strong, but like concrete it cracks, it's fixable

The foundation is going to populate not depopulate, it is going to survive by any means

The foundation will pass on more than money, it will pass on information

The foundation will be proud and overjoyed to see things going in the right direction.

Chapter 1 Born with It (Disability)

One in twenty-six people will develop epilepsy in their lifetime, and anyone can develop it. What happens during a seizure differs from person to person. However, each person has stereotypic seizures. Sixty-five million people in the world have epilepsy. Of those, three million live in the United States. One-third of people with epilepsy live with uncontrollable seizures because no available treatment works for them. Six out of ten people do not know the cause. I have been struggling with seizures all my life. I was two years old when my parents first realized I was an epileptic.

Limits are often due to lies about access to resources. Resources are available, but you may not have access to them. Society portrays that they have the resources to help people like me, but they

Darnelle Beckford

fail when challenged to help. Different people face these challenges even into adulthood.

Fear, Disability, and Options

When I was a baby in my crib and my mom heard me crying, she and my dad did not know what was going on with me. They knew I would not stop crying and they decided to take me to a doctor. Several tests were administered, and the results came back to confirm that I was an epileptic. Now, as a parent or sibling, imagine being advised by a medical professional that your son's cognitive brain function is damaged and to be prepared to care for your child for the rest of your life. Imagine being informed that due to this condition, your son will only be able to function with mental tasks that require the usage of his fingers and a wheelchair. This was upsetting news for my family as well as me.

From that day, our lives would be changed forever due to the type of impact that seizures would have on me and my family mentally, emotionally, and physically. My parents were more fearful. I did not care about the difference. I was more frustrated. I was a happy child and full of energy. I cared about being a child.

I was first introduced to my neurologist, Dr. Jayoung Pak whose office was in Newark, NJ. I was put on multiple medications, and some medicine would make me sleepy. Having seizures often slowed down

Let's Be Realistic

my learning development. I was not learning as fast as the other kids in school, and I felt dumb. This did not bother me as much until I got older. There were times I would have to either repeat classes and grade levels or be taken out of school due to my learning disability. As for my family, some of them did not want to be with or around me due to my seizures and found it more convenient to not deal with me.

As a kid, I did not care that I had seizure episodes. I remember being in school (in 1998) and it was gym time. I had to be about 9 years old at the time. We were playing baseball inside the school, and I was on first base and one of my classmates at the time was at bat. I fell to the floor and all I remembered was waking up to the school nurse calling my name. I woke up to the entire gym class sitting and waiting for my episode to pass. The school called my daddy, and I told him what happened. Normally, when I have seizures, I would blackout, go to sleep, and rely on bystanders to tell me what happened.

After each episode, I would have blackouts and go right to sleep. This would happen numerous times, but I would go on about my day as a kid. Each time this happens, it takes a toll on my parents and family present at the time of seizure. When I knew it would happen, I would run to my mother or father and they would try to console me. It would take a special toll on my mother, and she would end up losing

Darnelle Beckford

weight. Working 16-hour long shifts and then taking me to my doctors' visit put added stress on my mother.

Growing with a Disability

As I got older, it would affect me more differently than it would as a kid. In 2005, I was 16 at the time and I was at my uncle's house because my parents were away. My aunt had to pick me up and bring me to their house because my parents did not want me to be alone. To most kids, that would be a dream, but for me, it was not because of my seizures. No one wanted me to be alone by myself, so back to my uncle's house, I went.

I had just come home from school that day. I decided to go to the basement to sleep on the couch. When I woke up, my cousin Shantel was right in front of me and saying to me, "you must be really tired". I said yes, and that is all I remembered. Next, the EMTs were putting a breathing mask on me due to my cousin's grandmother calling 911. I spent all day and half the night at the hospital where my uncle stayed with me until I was discharged.

The next episode occurred a couple of months later. During this episode, I rolled out of my bed onto the floor on my weights and smashed my lip on the weights. It was so bloody that my mother had to clean me up and put me back into bed. She laid next to me. That same night, I had another one but this time, my mother was next to me when it happened.

The next day, I had school, and everyone asked me what happened, and I lied and said I got beaten up because I hated explaining what happened to everyone. Most people would ask why, and I would never answer because I was embarrassed, and I would not know how to explain what really happened to my face.

After that episode, I went on for 6-7 years without having any seizure episodes. During that time, I finally got my driver's license which was a big deal to me, and I was so excited about it.

What I Learned

Resources must be applied to mental health as well as physical and emotional health. Focus on advantages. The journey that you are on may be difficult but stay on the course. Things will get better. I am proud of myself and the person I have become, and my family is the reason. What we went through as a family did not only bring us closer, but my family grew more understanding of me and my disability and how to deal with it regularly. This was something they struggled with before we became closer.

Several people need to hear my story. I believe my story will inspire others who are going through the same things I went through

Darnelle Beckford

and even worse. I have been in and out of hospitals as a child, with only my parents trying to figure out how to control my seizures. I have gone through a series of tests that involved devices and cables connected to my head wrapped with a bandage. I have been embarrassed to the point of holding my head down. I had to lift my head and find the strength to pursue my dreams. Along the way, I gained confidence through my experiences. My approach was not tactical. It was strategic. Rather than fighting their narrative, I decided to spend my energy showing them.

Application to You

I found that my disability was the source of my challenges. People around me took my protection farther than I wanted. If you face a similar situation, do not spend time arguing or complaining about how you are being treated. Work within the space you are provided. Work in secret if you must. Achieve beyond what they think you can do. As they come along with their praise, don't get caught up even then. Continue to execute your strategic plan. Change the narrative so much that you become the standard rather than the exception. Beat the odds as a matter of principle. Know that others are inspired by your struggles, your perseverance, your advancement, and your achievement. You are not being greedy when you want more. You are

Let's Be Realistic

living your best life. You are not being unrealistic. You are creating new realities.

Darnelle Beckford

Chapter 2 From Disadvantages to Advantages

Society cares about your disadvantages. But they diminish the possibilities of a person with a disability. I want people to know that I own my disabilities, and I am no less capable compared to the average person. I must constantly prove myself. I must work 20 times harder than a person who has nothing noticeably wrong with them. I just want a chance. Give me the chance to prove myself. I can do what you think I cannot do. Thankfully, the lack of belief has resulted in more motivation for me to succeed.

I will not lie. I have some resentment. The expectations for me were not as high as they should have been. The bar was too low. I was much more than a high school diploma and a retail job. I decided to look at colleges including community college. I pushed to achieve beyond what others held for me. I had to raise the standard for myself. I had to set a new bar for myself.

Most Likely to Fail

Seizures were the cause of my learning disability, causing challenges for me in school. I was transferred from a catholic school to the public school system. I remained in the special education program for the rest of my secondary education. My father was a strong advocate for me academically and he realized that the school I was attending was not the best learning environment for me.

I was set up for failure. I felt like I was unwanted. I had to promote the idea that I deserved to be here. Too many believe that some kids cannot handle certain things. They tell some children that they cannot handle certain circumstances. They know what the child is good at and what they are not good at, but many seem not to believe that the child can learn and develop like other children. Often, they can. I could. They were right that I had challenges, but that just meant that I needed to hear it in a different way.

Special education classes seemed different for me and was a complete culture shock. The teaching style and the type of work was different from what I was accustomed to. The work I was given kept me in a box, but at the same time, it set me up for academic success.

Darnelle Beckford

The work they gave me included assignments about time management, balancing a checkbook, and other daily living skills. However, my sister's assignments looked completely different from mine. I often thought to myself that that is the kind of work I should be completing. Work that would prepare me for college and future life goals. Unfortunately, that was not the case for me.

One of my favorite artists goes by the stage name of Bounty Killer. His song, "All a Dream", is an inspiration to me. The lyrics in the song say:

> Not everything you can achieve in one go
> Somethings are very hard,
> But when you overcome that hurdle,
> You get a sense of real reward
> Even the greatest stumble
> But still do not let down your guard
> You got to motivate yourself elevate yourself
> No underestimate yourself, push yourself

What he is saying in this verse is that you may need to try more than once to get where you want to go. Your goals in life or career are not going to be easy. They will be hard. But once you apply perseverance and hard work, you are going to see the reward of your

Let's Be Realistic

labor. Even your favorite sports star, singer, and rapper had to climb their way to the top. Persevere. Keep going by motivating yourself. Keep learning. Know your value and add tax. Keep pushing. Things are coming your way sooner rather than later.

I take those lyrics to heart because there are so many times I want to give up in school and in other things, but I always tell myself not to give up. I often remind myself that I am trying to better my life and help others better themselves. Giving up now is not an option.

When I was 18 years old, I attended a school named New Road School. The school was equipped for students like me. I was moved from the high school side where I completed all the work that I needed to get done to move to the vocational technical side, where we would focus more on various career fields. Although they were intentionally exposing us to different career areas, I already knew that I wanted to go to college. I wanted to go to college to prove not only to myself but to my family and others that I was capable of excelling outside the box that I was put in based on my disability. Once I decided that I wanted to pursue college, there was no stopping me. I told myself there must be something else better for me besides sitting in a cube and doing computer work and assignments that had nothing to do with furthering my education for college. Completing tasks that I believed were not beneficial bothered me greatly. I decided to share

Darnelle Beckford

my thoughts with one of my teachers, Mrs. Stacy Kentrus. We had a long conversation about my expectations for myself, as well as her expectations for me, and agreed we would not accept anything less.

True to Bounty Killer's words, I had to repeat with Mrs. Kentrus. I told my parents that I wanted to graduate with my original graduating class, but due to being in special education my expected or assigned graduation date per the school district was 2010. My parents were in favor of me graduating with the assigned graduating date and felt that would better prepare me. I agreed on the condition that I stay in Mrs. Kentrus' class.

The educational system is flawed. I am not sure that anyone disagrees with that statement. But let us be clear about what the most insidious flaw is. Schools focus on the deficiencies and the challenges of the students more than the abilities, opportunities, and strengths. There is nothing wrong with identifying weaknesses to address them. The resources and proper tools should be provided to address those weaknesses. The same energy toward resources and tools should be provided to enhance the strengths of each student.

I have a unique perspective influenced by experience with special education and mainstream education. The challenge is that special education, created with a recognition of the special needs and disabilities, seemed less prepared to address deficiencies and enhance

Let's Be Realistic

strengths. The goal seemed to be management rather than inspiration. For example, I was a good cook. I was presented with the options for employment and application of culinary skills. But I was not provided an expanded view of the foodservice industry, hospitality and tourism, franchising, and business management.

Defining Myself

Another of my favorite musicians is Tupac. He writes lyrics that you must return to again and again. You must grab books to decipher what he is talking about at a deeper level. Obtaining my driver's license was deeper than it seemed. It was more than an achievement beyond what others thought was impossible. It was a confirmation that I was in control of my own life. The levels I would reach were up to me and my perseverance to achieve.

One of my favorite quotes from Tupac is, "Life is a wheel of fortune, and it's my turn to spin it." He means that life is yours and you must choose to contribute to society. You determine what you contribute. I have a story to tell. I am more than what you can see. I am more than a young, Black, male. I am not limited by what others perceive.

The question was whether I could handle it. My version was, "How could I know if I could handle it if I have never tried." Even though you have a disability, you also have abilities. I always had something to prove. I do not know if it was the stigma, but I was motivated to act and try.

I am reminded of the show 911. Heady, a character in the show, said, "I am tired of having to prove myself to everyone. I am tired of having to prove to everyone that I can do this." It stuck with me because this is how I feel. I get tired, but I also need to speak up because others find themselves in this same situation. They must prove that they can do the task—that they deserve to be in the room. Society does not readily accept certain people.

I always wanted to prove myself. People suggest that college is not for everybody. That may be true. But it was for me because I did not have the luxury of a legacy handed down to me. I knew that I had to build something from little. I built and am still building from a simple opportunity.

I am determined. That is something that people who know me know about me. I will finish what I start if it is within my power. A lot of people did not think I could finish high school or college. Every time I make the dean's list, it was a significant accomplishment in the minds of others. But for me, it was the result of consistent work. The bar was set low for me, but I set my own bar. If I did not achieve what I set out to achieve, I considered it a failure. But I collected myself, examined what I did, and reorganized how to go after the next opportunity.

Let's Be Realistic

What I Learned

"Amid the chaos, there is always opportunity."

You must advocate for yourself. That is the one thing about me. I do not like to be handed anything. Even though the law supports the reality that I can receive special treatment, I never wanted to be the person that was defined by the extra time or other accommodations. I worked hard to see that people see me as normal. I worked my butt off to make sure people see that. That is my default position, but I must also balance that with seeking help for those things that I find difficult. Advocacy requires you to be adamant – not so much with accommodations, but with explaining to people who observe the help you receive.

Your awareness is both of self and society—your rights and access to privileges. Most people think of disabled as physically disabled. You must know your limitations and what is helpful for you. I was nervous to ask for help, but I was never afraid. They could say no, yes, or figure it out on your own. Your job is to create your own model for receiving help and experiencing help. That openness and awareness create the reciprocity that encourages people to ask and receive help from me.

Darnelle Beckford

Application for You

You may need to set your own system of production, motivation, and achievement. You may not have people who give you much, train you, or provide an example nearby. You may need to conduct your own research and find these people beyond your inner circle. I had to create my own mission. If you are like me, refuse to allow the system to define you, who you are, or what you are capable of. When they see you, they see you as inferior or like something is wrong with you. You may have challenges, but you have abilities too.

The Individualized Education Program (IEP) is a legal plan with the purpose of creating an individualized education plan for each student. It's called a program because the plan is not just about education. It describes a system of support for the student incorporating parents as well.

It seems that special education only focuses on IEPs that limit students. They limit the level of exposure that is provided for the students. Many IEPs are supposed to be strength-based and look at abilities and limitations. A strength-based IEP often boils down to a shift in mindset. The process must be reformed to increase exposure, make lessons realistic and experiential, and engage students in real environments. This would be a positive step for every student. Know your capabilities and build on them. Everything will work out as you

Let's Be Realistic

commit to growth and development. Build based on students' capabilities and interests. Determine how strengths might be used to set goals that address particular needs and aspirations of each student.

The system never really focused on my true potential and what I could do. They should have asked me, the student, what I wanted or needed to learn, what would be beneficial for me later in life, and what dreams I held. Instead, they asked questions just to place me and others in a box of mediocrity, a confined and lonely space defined by the limitations existing primarily in their own heads. Think twice, ask more, and do the research. Listen to those like me who have been through it and have made a career out of proving doubters wrong.

Darnelle Beckford

THE FOUNDATION WOMAN PT2

By Darnelle Beckford

Inspired by "God is Love" from Popcaan and Beres Hammond

The foundation woman will give you what you need not what you want

The foundation woman will fight with you to take on the world

The foundation woman will not be with you for opportunity but create her own

The foundation woman will make your weakness your strength

The foundation woman will build with you, not take from you

The foundation woman will not let outsiders into the relationship and have a say so

The foundation woman will teach you and show you how to invest your money

The foundation woman will teach you more about yourself

Chapter 3 Friendship, Acceptance or Not

As a little boy, I was so embarrassed by how I looked with cables and wires attached to me. I would stay home until it was time to go back to the neurologist. As a child and up to adulthood, I would be depressed thinking I would never be able to live a normal life because of these seizures. I would have thoughts about how people would accept me, especially women that I would date or marry. I would have to tell each one my secret, which would be my seizures. I hate telling people about it. Even now, I must completely trust and feel comfortable before sharing my medical condition.

Acceptance

I questioned whether friends would accept me. It took me a while to tell my best friends even though they understand my

Darnelle Beckford

condition and love me regardless. I still get worried about how they would see me. How will they react if I were to have an episode? I never wanted to receive special treatment because of my disability. I wanted to be treated just like everyone else and I fought hard to be treated the same way. I get reminded every day about my medical condition just by looking at the medicine bottles in my room and the frequent doctor visits. The frequency of the visits depends on the frequency of my seizures. With my disability constantly in the forefront of my mind, when I attend classes in college, I believe I must work a hundred times more than the average student. I have a lot to prove not only to myself but to others. To show that no matter what comes my way, I can and will overcome. I can overcome any obstacle because I am determined, passionate, and dedicated.

The simple things the everyday child, teenager, or even adult takes for granted, I did not; I found joy. Getting a car, driver's license, a job, getting into college, in my mind, was a great accomplishment. But the thoughts of how I would explain my medical condition to my unknown future wife and kids or new associates still plagued my mind. This troubled me greatly because I saw how my condition about my everyday life and safety placed a weight of worry on my family when I was trying to live my best life. Sometimes, I feel I would not be successful because of my seizures, but my neurologist thought differently.

Let's Be Realistic

My neurologist, at the time, was Dr. Jayoung Pak at the University of Medicine and Dentistry in New Jersey. She installed a vagus nerve stimulator, a device with a magnet. In the event of a seizure episode, I had to swipe the magnet across my chest and the seizures would stop, but it would cause me to cough heavily. The device was placed in my chest with wires leading into my brain where all the seizure activity occurred. Every 7-10 years, depending on the battery life of the stimulator, I would have to get the battery changed, and that would require surgery again. They would cut the same scar and it would take long to heal, and when it healed, it would not heal to my liking. From then, the surgeries would continue. The scars would remain the same, big, long – a constant reminder of my private pain.

I was the first kid to have that particular surgery. I was about 6-8 years old. Even though the surgery was a success, I would still have a scar on my chest and neck for the rest of my life. Naturally, people would ask me how I got the scar, and I would tell them different stories on how I got it. Honestly, I did not want to tell them the real story. I would be embarrassed to take off my shirt or to do any activity where my chest would be exposed. I would do anything and everything to hide my scars because I was so uncomfortable and insecure about my scars.

Darnelle Beckford

Romantics

I am still afraid of letting people know about my disability. I do not know how they will react. I have met people and shared. I have watched as they distanced themselves and fell away not wanting the responsibility for me. As a result, I am slow to open to people. I am much more of an observer. Accepting myself is tied to this experience of being accepted by others. As a friend, I am open, loyal, and confidant. I keep my friend circle to a limited number knowing that I have a level of acceptance and support from each of them. The people I call friends look out for me. My siblings look out for me like extensions of my parents. Whether it is a new job, borrowing money, or anything else, they offer an acceptance. That is support at its core. They offer a safe space to be me to explore the world, my challenges, and my successes. They inspire me to accept myself without reservation.

I want a Foundational woman, not an Opportunity woman. I want someone I can build with, not someone who is there for the opportunity of being married, getting money, or using me. I want a person who gives me what I need versus what I want and vice versa. A person who gives you what you need will never outstretch their value. A person who gives you what you want will eventually expend their usefulness.

Let's Be Realistic

When you engage with a person who has a disability, the motivations must be pure. Sure, that is true in all relationships, but I want to emphasize it for relationships with persons with disabilities. You have additional challenges, for example with my seizures. With me, the fear is that during relationships, including hanging out, an episode may occur, and those around me may not know how to deal with it. Intimacy could trigger an episode. Another challenge is maintaining memories. I may forget something I was told five minutes ago. I typically require multiple reminders. The short-term daily tasks can slip my mind quickly. It can be a source of stress for me and others.

The solution is simple. I inform the friends I hang with about techniques and the best approach to my episodes. The woman I relate to must know what the challenges are and have strategies to deal with them. This is no different than living with any other individual. In that way, I am like any other person. For example, if a person has heart disease or asthma and they know about it, they can let their partner know and plan for the chance that an episode may interrupt their lives. I do not allow epilepsy to define me, but I do plan as if episodes may occur.

Darnelle Beckford

I treat women with respect, but some did not have the tools to reciprocate that care. Just as I am, I worked to address my physical health and advance my cognitive health. A woman must address her health. I do not know if the stress is more when a disability is present. I believe that stress has different features. Managing the breaking points relating to this stress is critical to healthy relationships.

Metaphorically, I built the table from scratch. I want my wife to be the tablecloth and the centerpiece that demonstrates that we created the scene together. Marriage must be that partnership between two people—the two against the world. We are the person we need, not just the person we want.

What I Learned

I will not lie. I was terrified about telling people about my disability and epilepsy. I did not want to be looked at differently. I would pull them aside one by one so as not to have a group challenge in addition to the anxiety of revealing myself. I was shocked each time to be accepted. Telling secrets like these risks being disowned. I thought they would not want to talk or hang with me anymore. I was open-minded and accepting of them and saw that reciprocated. Nothing was off-limits to us after that. Our bond was stronger than it

Let's Be Realistic

was before. I observed that they opened more. They shared their struggles.

I had always been the guy that my female friends could talk to without the fear of being mistreated, stalked, or hit on. They could talk to me about school, work, significant others, and their personal lives. My openness motivated their openness. I respected them and they respected me.

I am open to a romantic relationship. I am still afraid. I do not know how that person will react to my specific disabilities. That acceptance question still lingers for me. I do not know that anyone would want to take on that stress. I do not want to be alienated from a romantic relationship. I do not want to be in a relationship based on pity or curiosity about my disability. The thoughts are stressful. The person I connect with must understand that my disability comes with the relationship package. I have experienced letdown – someone says they will stand by me and they later changed their mind. When they leave after learning of my disabilities, my fears are reinforced. I am not fearful of being alone. I look forward to building a solid foundation with someone I can call my wife and soulmate.

Darnelle Beckford

Application for You

Tyler Perry shared this analogy of the tree. People are like leaves, branches, or roots. He suggests that you find people who are roots. Leaves will leave. Branches are just connections. Be careful and identify the roots—those who will be there for the long term.

I am want to find a woman who will be a root to my tree. As Shakespeare wrote in King Lear:

The wheel is come full circle, I am here.

Relationships must be like Gucci Mane and his wife. He gave her $100,000. She took the money and built a business grossing $100 million per year. That is the type of woman I desire. I want to connect, grow, and thrive with someone.

I had (and might still have) an insecurity that keeps me from reaching out and being comfortable in relationships. The key to working past this is to connect with people who are genuine, kind, and accepting. You can both live with your insecurity and work through your insecurity with a person like that. You will find many people who will seek to tease you or bully you in your insecurity. Take their power away. Take your power back by accepting your weaknesses and making them into strengths. The things you cannot change about yourself must become simple traits, not downfalls, shame, or

Let's Be Realistic

problems. Accept them for what they are. Work to improve. Stand tall knowing who you are, and work towards the impact you want to have on the world.

Darnelle Beckford

Only in relationship can you know yourself, not in abstraction and certainly not in isolation. The movement of behavior is the sure guide to yourself. It's the mirror of your consciousness; this mirror will reveal its content, the images, the attachments, the fears, the loneliness, the joy, and sorry. Poverty lies in running away from this, either in its sublimations or its identities.

JIDDU KRISHNAMURTI

Section II: My Way Forward

Darnelle Beckford

Chapter 4 Community College

My sister was preparing for post-secondary education by visiting various universities. I was secretly taking notes with a burning desire to share the same experience. When it was time for my high school graduation before my sister left for college, I informed my parents that I wanted to attend college and move on like my friends. Reluctantly, my parents told me that college was not made for everyone. I expressed my desire to be successful to my parent, and I did not want to allow my learning disability to define me or keep me from succeeding. I thought about college before I went on the college visits with my sister. I wanted to expand my mind and learn about new things. What I learned through those experiences was critical. I observed and soaked up what I saw like a sponge. I listened to the experiences of my mother who also attended community college.

Let's Be Realistic

In 2010, I realized I was really going to have to work hard and apply myself to be ready for the rigor of college. I planned to continue to work hard and stay focused as I began to approach graduation. I begin to search for schools that would be a good fit for me personally and meet my academic and professional needs. The first school I identified was Full Sail University (F.S.U.). F.S.U was a school that had a strong program for individuals pursuing arts and media. I really wanted to go there because I love music and I wanted to be in the music business.

My dad and I got on a plane and flew to Florida for the weekend. I really loved the school, but I had to keep the door open. The next school I visited was Beacon College and it was the same structure as New Road, the high school that I attended. It was a college created for people who were accustomed to a special education structure. I did not want to attend Beacon College because it reminded me of my former high school. I did not feel that I could mentally take a similar environment like New Road High.

My Determination

Although I did not choose the two schools I visited, I decided to choose the community college route. On the first day of class, my dad called me on the phone and stated how much he was proud of me

Darnelle Beckford

for taking the step to better myself. He told me that not a lot of people would go to great lengths to achieve what I had achieved.

While I attended a community college, I pursued a degree in food and beverage management. While I was there, I made the dean's list on several occasions. This was a big thing not only to me but to my family as well. Every time I receive a letter from the school, I would never open it; I would hand it to my parents and one of them would open and read the letter. They would be so happy; whereas it did not mean anything to me because I knew I could do it. I saw myself making the dean's list from the first time I started college. I stayed focused on my schoolwork and I did not let anything distract me from my academic goal.

Graduation and a Toast

It happened. In the summer of 2015, all the hard work while both working at a hospital, attending school, and balancing a relationship, I finally graduated! Graduating and achieving something a lot of people said that I could not do was self-satisfying.

My parents, my sister, my godmother, and my aunt, who came from Jamaica, were there to witness this milestone. Even though I did not graduate with honors, something that I always desired, I graduated with a GPA of 3.0. A 3.0 was good enough by other standards, but not my own; however, it still was a blessing. When I

Let's Be Realistic

finally received my graduating card and handed it to the announcer, my name was called and you could hear my entire family cheering, "YES!! Darney!" The truth of the matter is that I did not hear them, but I could see and hear the people that doubted me for my decision to pursue college with a learning disability. The challenges and setbacks that could have stopped me, pushed me to succeed. I kept on defying the odds against me and it was a great feeling.

After graduation, we headed back to my house, where my friends and family would gather to celebrate my achievements. I remember specifically the speech my godfather made at the celebration. He said "not a lot of people could have gone through what you did and come out with a degree. Even though it's an associate degree, you still got a college degree, and not a lot of people in your condition can say or do that, but you did". At the end of his heartfelt speech, everyone raised their glasses to toast me.

I remember sharing with my godfather a week prior, that I was scared because I felt I was going to fail somehow. I did not believe I was going to fail due to being a Jamaican-American, but having a disability tag associated with me, I was not sure how the world was going to view me. Would they see an educated man with a disability or a young man who worked hard and earned his degree against all odds? Regardless, how they view me really does not matter. The key is believing and encouraging yourself to know that you can do it. Yes,

Darnelle Beckford

I will be positive throughout this whole process on which we call life and these roads and streets we call journey. Always remember to stay the course because the journey will get easier and with it comes something called success. I would hear people talk about it like celebrity athletes say it all the time and I thought it was all a hype, but success is real.

What I Learned

The single most important task in any situation is to ask questions. We have all heard the phrase, "Knowledge is power." It has become cliché. But it is true. No question is dumb. Even if it is considered dumb, it still needs to be asked. People are afraid to ask a question because asking attracts attention. As you know, most people in the room want to know the answer to the question being asked, no matter how dumb others think the question is. Sometimes, I ask questions that I think are stupid. The person I am asking often tells me that the question is not dumb, it takes the concept in a different direction. I have had teachers tell their colleagues about the quality of my questions. "That is a good question, Darnelle. I never thought of it in that way."

Most of the time, you ask questions to get an answer right away. You may take that answer and move forward. I ask different people the same questions but in different contexts. I want to create

Let's Be Realistic

knowledge and understanding. Knowledge comes from asking questions. Understanding comes from processing multiple answers in different contexts. I feel, often, we do not listen to answers with a view of how to appropriately utilize them. Discourse is limited because we have trouble asking questions and being challenged by the answers.

Questions communicate intelligence. Sometimes, I surprise myself when reviewing the answers I received from teachers, classmates, and others. Communication through questions and follow-up questions creates a richer and more vibrant interaction. You will be considered intelligent based on the questions you ask and the quality of the interactions you can create.

Application for You

The lesson for you is to realize the challenge of asking for help. The pressure to be perceived as normal and typical is intense. But you must be you. If you are different, so be it. No matter the accommodations you receive, what defines you is what you create and the person you are. If you are limited by a disability, an addiction, or something else, change your mindset from a focus on what you cannot do. Release yourself from dependence or blame of a flawed system. Focus instead on your strengths. Nurture them like plants and watch them flourish. Address your limitations with resources and

Darnelle Beckford

tools. Take the time to develop in those areas through learning, help seeking, and practice. When you fall, get back up. Feel the embarrassment if it comes, but never isolate yourself based on what you have been through.

Kevin Hart is one of my greatest inspirations. He worked from being unknown to becoming a megastar. He sold out Madison Square Garden multiple times. That is impressive. But his greatest inspiration to me are the people around him that he propelled to greatness. They benefitted from his success, addressed their limitations, and enhanced their strengths.

Often, you stubbornly refuse help when offered. Yet this is the first requirement of being a helper. You must understand what it is to receive help. Help did not come easily for me. I had to speak up and ask for it. Laws exist for people who are in wheelchairs or otherwise physically challenged. Those same rules are supposed to apply to people with other disabilities, but it is not always readily given when your disability is invisible. In these situations, you must become aware, be articulate, and adamant.

Asking is difficult, but if you are not willing to ask for help, you will not succeed. People may be willing to help, but they are not willing to help you 100%. They may want you to be more self-sufficient. They may withhold out of envy or not wanting you to surpass them. They

Let's Be Realistic

may not understand how to effectively help. Your task is to communicate directly and ask your questions with specificity and clarity.

Darnelle Beckford

Chapter 5 My Darkest Moments

It was 2013 and my cousin Tara was coming up from Jamaica. It was her first trip to America. My parents went to a party and they told me that I should go to the mall with my cousin, my Godfathers wife, his nephew, and kids. I went to the mall, there was no problem. When we were driving back from the mall, I decided to take a short nap. I woke up and had an episode. It was a big one. My cousin freaked out because she had never seen me have a seizure. My mother was notified, and my cousin tried to get me to go to the hospital, but I refused. I did agree to be dropped off at my godfather's house to wait for my parents.

While I was waiting for my parents, all I could think about was losing my freedom to drive and a whole bunch of things that came along with it. This made me depressed, and I did not want to go with my family thinking that I would be a burden. I would stay in the house and sit in my own funk.

Depression

I lost my license for six months and at the time, I was still attending community college. I had to be transported back and forth to school by mom, dad, and family friends. At the time, I was completing my Associate degree in food and beverage management. Some of my coursework involved going to another school for classes. Imagine having to depend on others when you are used to depending on yourself to get around. It was an annoying and frustrating time for me to say the least.

There were more seizures to follow. After each episode. I would find myself spiraling deeper into depression. My parents suggested that I talk to someone because I had done this previously while in school, so I agreed.

My therapist helped me out a lot in dealing with the depression and anger I was feeling. People tried to be supportive and attempt to cheer me up as much as they could, but they really did not understand my battle. Although I felt like no one could understand, I had to take a step back and see that my parents were going through the same thing, but differently. They had to deal with their son being

Darnelle Beckford

impacted by this condition and could not do anything about it but stand by my side and do their very best, which they did.

Never Give Up

I did not know what it meant until I understood. I now understand where people are coming from when they say, "Never give up!" I have heard athletes, business leaders, and others talk about this concept. They did not always strike me as authentic.

We must educate ourselves and our children in the rich fields of knowledge which others have used.
Elijah Muhammad

I have found a way out of my dull moments with the purpose to support others. I was a part of a mentorship program when I was in high school. I did not know what to say when I began. I did not want to share my whole story with a person that I had never met. I found that the quote of Elijah Muhammad was the way: Education. Educate people to the reality of their experience. Give them knowledge. The knowledge builds the opportunity for a different perspective beyond despair and low expectations. Educate the people who do not know.

I am still fearful for the future. It may be insecurity. I am sure that it is. I worry about connecting with a woman and falling in love

Let's Be Realistic

and having to inform her about my disability. I am afraid of having children who may also have the same disability. I know that I can educate them on what to do. I can share my story and how I overcame my challenges. I can demonstrate to anyone who will listen that you may have things that you cannot do, but you have a longer list of things that you can do. You can accomplish at levels like others and beyond those who refuse to apply themselves.

The following week after the episode with my cousin, I went to see a new neurologist. It was a challenge to trust someone new with my disability and care. My mom, dad, and I were talking with the nurse about my history. I was stressed. I had an episode. During the episode, the neurologist spoke three words. "Apple. Banana. Orange." He spoke to them to determine whether I remembered anything. When I was a kid, I would blackout during my episodes and not remember anything. He demonstrated that as I was getting older, I was retaining awareness during the episodes. This was an encouraging development as my parents and I were looking for any good news we could get.

My dad had been reading about a surgery that could relieve me of the seizures for life. It was a laser surgery performed by a robot. It requires removal of the skull and targeted laser therapy into the part of the brain that is active during seizures. We brought the article up to

Darnelle Beckford

the neurologist. However, the neurologist informed, "in order to be eligible for the surgery, he must fail every medication."

Of course, at that point, I had multiple medications, but I had not experienced every medication. I was devastated. I knew I could not go through all medications from lowest to highest doses. The hope was that I would not need medication. I hoped and prayed that this would free me up to do what other people do. I could drink alcohol, for example, without worrying about side effects or interactions with the medication. There was nothing I could do about it. I had to roll with the punches. The consolation was that I was put on a new medication that seemed to help. I can never get used to daily medication, but I have accepted that this is how I maintain my health.

What I Learned

Some people will count me out. My disability will threaten to take me out. But grace applies to both situations. I apply grace to people when they come back realizing that they were not supportive. They see me succeed and sometimes find the courage to apologize. I accept their apologies without ridicule or reservation. I use their disbelief as fuel. I thank them for gassing me. I apply grace also when my disability takes me into depression and self-doubt. I refuse to lower my expectations for myself while also managing my illness as it comes.

Let's Be Realistic

I am reminded of the story of Chicken Little. This little chicken saw that the sky was falling, and no one believed him. He was vindicated when the sky eventually fell. My success is coming and indeed has already come. I do not need to proclaim it from rooftops or convince people. They will see it when it comes and recognize that I am no prophet. I am simply a hard worker who decided to believe in himself, overcome depression when it comes, and succeed as my only option.

Application for You

Don't follow the non-believers. Whether it is on social media, face-to-face interactions, or in other forms. Try. Learn. Retry. Relearn. Diversify. Keep moving forward, progressing, and trying. That is all a successful life is: Consistency. As you are consistent, do your best to reach out, reach back, and help others persevere.

While I was attending High Road school, I was put in a position of mentoring kids younger or the same age as myself who just wanted to be heard and wanted someone to talk to. That was the first step of being in a leadership-type position and with that, I gradually took the step. This position was given to me in the last two years I was there. It was also a step for me from being a follower to a leader.

Darnelle Beckford

Believe it or not, you can learn a lot about the person you follow and you want to be their kind of leader. I had to learn that for myself. With that, I was implanting positivity into others and into myself. I did that for a while until I graduated. That is why I will always help those who want help but do not have the financial means. I have a desire to support, encourage, motivate, and inspire people; I guess that is just the mentor in me. I want to see people succeed and for them to realize their full potential.

Chapter 6 Make it with Help from Friends

I decided to take some time off after community college, but not too much because I did not want to forget everything I learned. After working for a while and going through relationship problems, I set a timetable for myself to start school again. I started researching schools around my area and I found Berkeley College. After reviewing the website, I visited the school. There was something about Berkley College that reminded me of my high school. It was the small school setting and small classrooms. Small classrooms made class interaction more personable, and I felt this was a setting that would be best for me at the time.

Making it with Friends

In the winter of 2017, I started my first semester where I majored in business management. Just like any other first day, I felt

Darnelle Beckford

nervous and shy. I tend to want to get to know a person better initially before opening up to people. I did not click with anybody there. There were people I was cool with and got to know, but it was not like we were going to be friends for life. Until I met one of my best friends who is like a baby sister to me; her name is Marylin. Marylin and I were in the same statistics class. I initially did not say anything to Marylin until a couple of classes later in the semester. That is when we started to get to know each other, and we exchanged numbers. We began to have more classes together which allowed us to become even closer.

It took me a while to share my secret of having seizures with Marylin because that is something that I was not ready to disclose. Not knowing how people would view me or treat me due to my illness made it difficult for me to readily share. When I did share it with her, to the best of my knowledge she took it as if it was nothing to her. She also shared some personal stuff with me which I will never tell. After our conversation, we started spending time together outside of school and we became close friends. We would talk on the phone for hours and spend time at each other's house and share some of our deepest secrets.

The following semester my baby sister introduced me to Krystal, who would soon become my other sister and best friend. I was shy and did not know her, but after being around her and feeling comfortable around her, we became close. Krystal was crazy but at the same time you could have a serious conversation with her, and she was a down-to-earth type of girl. Right after meeting Krystal, I was introduced to my other best friend and second youngest sister, Kiara. Kiara, who is a proud spiritual person, was the final piece to our group. The friends that I was looking for all along, I finally found, or I should say, we found each other.

Each day, we would find new things to talk about and we would motivate, inspire, and empower each other to do better whether it was in school, work, or everyday life. They are not just best friends, but my sisters, and like sisters, they are very protective of me and they truly care for me as much as I care for them. We are all about being positive and getting the best out of each other and pushing each other. We go through a lot in our personal lives, but at the end of the day, we get through it. We give each other advice daily, and we pick each other up when the times get rough. We celebrate each other's birthdays, hang out, and share our secrets. When it comes to us, our life is an open book.

What I Learned

I paid my way through college starting with community college. I made sacrifices for the school I wanted to go to, but that allowed me to do things the right way. I was used to getting the short end of the

Darnelle Beckford

stick, but I always put myself in the best position to succeed. I completed college and started a career. My goal now is to build more on that foundation.

College was a challenge, to say the least. I applied myself in a way that I had never done before. The speeches about college life, what to be aware of, what to be focused on were few and far between. I had to give those speeches—find that insight—for myself. My father told me how proud he was and admitted that he did not think I would get that far. I told my mom about my plan to start my own business. She revealed that she was proud because I achieved a bachelor's degree—something she never expected. After achieving that, my family knew that I will do anything. They knew that I would apply myself to anything that I did.

Application for You

No matter what you are going through, there is no such thing as too much support. Love, support, and a personal relationship with God are key factors. Once you develop a personal relationship with God, you will see a lot of changes, not only in your behavior, but in the friends you have around you. That is why I choose the friends I have around me; filled with positive vibes and good energy. I am so grateful

Let's Be Realistic

to have my family and friends to help me get through some rough times and rejoice with me when I celebrate the good times.

You must commit yourself. Get a notebook or a digital file on your mobile device and write the pros and cons of whatever choices you want to make. You must study the cons and how to address them. Knowledge of the cons will be your greatest tool when challenges present themselves.

Another important consideration is your WHY. It has been said that a major in college is something that you want to do. A minor is something that you are interested in. I have always had an interest in business. I began in retail. That was one of my first jobs. I take the lessons and interests from that and apply them to my life, committing to continuous learning.

Take in everything that you can. You will be nervous at first. Be observant. Pay attention to the social interactions around you. Be open-minded and seek to learn from all angles. You never know what the knowledge is, where it will come from, and where it will take you.

Darnelle Beckford

I have loved. I have lost and I have changed. It has been difficult, but I have learned so much from it. I have learned that people can hurt you so deeply and not even worry about you. I learned that good people can change in a minute when their hearts have been broken. I've met great people, but mean people as well. But the most important thing I have learned is that every person in this world is strong enough to let go. People come and go and that's life! The most important thing is to stand up and realize that you deserve something better than a person who gives up on you.

SANJEET KUMAR

Section III: Mindset and Motivation

Darnelle Beckford

IM HERE FOR

By Darnelle Beckford

Inspired by "Leader" from Masicka and Dexta Daps

I'm here for advice
I'm here for my people
I'm here for those who care
I'm here for family and close friends
I'm here for those who are here for me
I'm here for those who are here for me
I'm here to shock and surpass expectation
I'm here for picking those up
I'm here for love, courage, commitment,
laughter, and friendship
I'm here for the truth
I'm here for passing on general information
I'm here for the right reasons not the wrong
And I'm here to stay

Chapter 7 Mindset Shift is Key

A good listener is a good learner. A good learner is a good earner.
Unknown

I look at celebrities and wonder if they will come back to the community to educate us. Will they simply come and talk to the kids for a one-time show, or will they commit to training others to follow in the footsteps of their success? I talk to kids and relate what I have been through. I share how I have overcome. I suggest that they find their own lessons within my story. Find what is similar, what is different, and how they may apply lessons to their own lives. You might not relate to everything, but you will find encouragement to make your own goals and achieve beyond what anyone thinks is possible.

Darnelle Beckford

Self-Esteem and Spirit

I was never a positive person earlier in my life, and early into my 20s, it took me a while to realize that for me to be positive and think positive, I had to do some major work on myself. Build my self-esteem. With all the struggles I have been through, it was time to make a change.

The first step in shifting your mindset is to improve self-esteem. You are powerful. You must know that. With the help of a trainer, named Mike, I started to exercise. He helped me realize the type of person I could be, and as I worked out, I saw a boost in my self-confidence. I began dating again after being single from a previous relationship that did not end well. Normally, I would dwell on it for a long time, trying to see what I did wrong, but seeing that I have been working on myself and my body, it did not affect me as much as it used to. At the same time, I got to know myself and realized what I was looking for in a woman and in any relationship.

I started doing a lot of positive things and the results led to more positive outcomes for my life. As a kid, I would go to church with my parents as well as any time I stayed with my Aunt in Mandeville, Jamaica. We would hold worship service in her living room before going to bed. I did not like the worship services because I never really had a personal relationship with God. As I got older, I started to understand and develop a personal relationship with God. When I

Let's Be Realistic

think about all the things my family and I have been through, I started to see the blessings and God's hand over my life.

Church was never really my thing, but I understand the importance of church and worship to God that has always been with me. I give thanks every day for my parents, family, and friends that continue to support me and give words of wisdom, real advice, and tough love even when I do not want to hear it.

Hope for Families

Any amount of hope must be expanded and nurtured. No matter how slim the chance, the movement must be to persevere. There is no other option. So, do it sustainably with love and optimism.

Fortunately, thanks to God, I was placed on a medication along with my original medication, and I have not had a seizure since then. Everything that I went through was not all bad; there were some good things I can remember. I just wanted to show everyone that I can do things on my own without anyone's help. I do not want people to believe that because of my disability, I am entitled to things. I wanted to show not only myself but others that a lot of things that you want will not be handed to you. At times, there will be struggles to reach your goals in life, but with hard work and dedication, you can do it as I did. The most important thing to do is to excel in the things you are good at and not hold back. Masicka, another dancehall artist that I

Darnelle Beckford

listen to, said, "you have to make it when you humble for sure." What he is saying is that whatever you want to become in life, you must always remain humble. When you are, good things will come to you when you least expect. Continue to work hard at it and stay grounded. In due time, things will happen.

The best advice I can give to parents going through the same situation my family and I went through is that it will get better with time. It may not seem like it at first, but it does if you have the right people in your corner. Moreover, staying positive with the right attitude and faith will go a long way. It does not matter what disease, disability, struggles, and life's pain that you are experiencing; do not let anybody tell you that you cannot do it. Whatever your dream or passion is, follow it. You will never know what the outcome is going to be. Do not wait for another minute or opportunity to pass you by and regret it later in life. Time will heal your wounds, your pain, and your fears, whether it be fear of not being accepted by others or fear of failure and not being the successful person that you imagine yourself to be. Do not worry, everything is going to work out just fine.

Without risk, there is no success, and without success, there would be no failure. Trust your instincts and the people that know you best. I had a lot more errors and setbacks earlier in my life and in the

Let's Be Realistic

middle of my life before things started to change for the better for me as a person and as a man.

> **If you don't have confidence in self, you are twice defeated in the race of life. With confidence, you have won even before you have started.**
> **Marcus Garvey**

What I Learned

Create a balance between receiving help and doing for yourself. When it comes to parents, you will have one parent who allows you to do whatever challenges you. You will have another parent who seeks to shelter you and keep you safe. The truth is that you will have this play out in relationships outside of your family. A person rarely knows how to balance help and your autonomy perfectly. Your job is to know your plans and your method to achieve them. In so doing, supportive relationships can work from your plan to provide information and other resources rather than starting from their own assumptions.

My motivation was to prove people wrong because of the limitations that I encountered. Even supportive people seemed to want me safe rather than want me to excel. I constantly saw myself in the position of self-motivation, to research for myself, challenge myself, and seek the basics, the nuances, and the advanced lessons. Action was my motivation. As I acted, I gained more momentum and that propelled me forward.

Application for You

You must discern between those moments when you are seeking validation and when you are seeking help. You must reduce your need for validation. It may never come in a way that supports your long-term growth and development. People may not provide the education and know-how you need. Some people will not have the experience that informs their approach to you. They may not know how to assess you properly. You will need to have this knowledge about yourself. Focus on help once you have exhausted your research. Ask for information but resist their opinions about whether you should or should not. Decide based on your research, not their support or lack of support.

Notice who is around you, what they are saying, and how independently you must work for your own self-esteem. Trust me, there is no better feeling when you work towards something after struggling for so long. In the process, you will learn patience and timing and how it will work in your favor later in life.

Let's Be Realistic

Hip hop legend and business mogul, 50 Cent, had a quote referring to school and the point of education. "If anything you needed was in the business class, there would be too many successful businesses." He's right. If the information was easy to access, the teacher would be too busy to teach a class. Create your own esteem, work ethic, and experience. Establish your own. That's Law 41 of the 48 Laws of Power.

The one thing I want to share with people is not just my story, but how I overcame so many obstacles in my life with a disability. I want to provide a message of hope and motivation, encouraging people that they can overcome anything in life if they remain humble, keep a positive mindset, and a close support system.

Darnelle Beckford

Chapter 8 Maintaining Me

I do not know. I guess you can call it a chip on my shoulder. Yet, I hinted at the beginning of the text, the chip on my shoulder regarding society and institutions was overcome through the support in my corner from immediate family, extended family, and friends that became family.

Gratitude

Nothing was handed to me. I had to work hard for it. I persevered through multiple struggles and forged my opportunity to succeed. I want to get back into my roots of mentoring kids with disabilities, home life challenges, and more of their struggles. My calling is to help. I also want to diversify to invest in several business ventures.

Let's Be Realistic

I should not be where I am, but I am here. I look at those who have a more physically limiting disability. I was surrounded, at times, by kids that had Down syndrome, speech problems, mobility challenges confined to wheelchairs. And then, there was me. I was in special education around them every day for years. I needed to leave or I would lose my mind. But I never treated those people any differently.

You do not have anything to be ashamed of. *The Art of War* speaks that the superior art of war is to win without fighting. I apply that. I disagree with all the people that look at me as weaker, fragile, or unintelligent. I show them through my achievement. I do not expend energy arguing about my ability. I use my energy to produce. This keeps me sane provides the energy to surpass expectations.

The Model

I will try. If I fail, I fail. But it will be because I tried and could not do it. Every day and every accomplishment is precious. Everything I have accomplished has been doubted by someone. I have come a long way and I am grateful for that. I take pride and encouragement in getting up and attending a 9 to 5 job even though it is not the career I will finally end up with. I consider it as an achievement to get to a point people believed I would never be.

Darnelle Beckford

Most people only know how to be in the limelight. They continue to make money. They do not share. My purpose is to create in the limelight, make money doing what I love, and share my process and the proceeds. People are not always willing to give help, but you always need help.

In the 48 laws of power, Law 11 is a follows:

> Learn to make people dependent upon you. Never teach people enough to have them become independent.

I want to change this mindset. I want to have a pipeline with the next person in line after me, supported by me.

For example, in the music industry, Rockafella Records was created by an artist, a marketer, and a musician. Rockawear came next. Rockafilms came later. The artists promoted after that success were the likes of Kanye West, Young Guns, J. Cole, and many others. The influence was not just the artists they touched. Those artists launched and supported other artists. Kanye's GOOD Music and J. Cole's Dreamville are launchpads in the industry.

I want my platform to help, launch, and support people. That is my calling. I am seeking it without hesitation.

Let's Be Realistic

My Model for Successful Living

1. Inspire You: Know that life has more to offer you than the average. I had to get the thoughts out of my head onto paper just like I had to seek out more information and move beyond the limitations of what people thought I could do. I believe everyone is born with this momentum, but it is worn down by the people you listen to and the choices you make.

2. Mold You: Know yourself. Be honest with yourself especially about what you want your life to be. Research yourself. Refuse to let people tell you what is possible even as they share the process. Go beyond their presentations to solve problems, answer questions, and create new opportunities for yourself.

3. Gather People Around You: Look for role models. Read about inspirational stories. Maintain a group of counselors, cheerleaders, and influencers. Gain strength, examples, and energy from these people.

4. Support Your Advancement and Achievement: The difference between the two is subtle but advance to keep moving toward your desired level of influence. That is creating a legacy. Achievement refers to the milestones along the way. Celebrate them briefly and gain motivation. Set them up as reminders for

Darnelle Beckford

those moments when you get discouraged. Remember that you can because you have.

What I Learned

I must do more than other people, but that is not because of my learning disability. That reality of doing more is because I want more from my life than the average. I want to have enough to reach back and influence others to live to their full potential. I decided that this will be my life, and it is up to me to reach those goals.

I see a new day. Young people are standing up and holding adults accountable for the decisions that they make and the types of leadership they provide. Our parents may not have taken a stand in the same way because of the perceived backlash. But we are not afraid in this generation. I foresee a future, 20 to 30 years from now, revealing the results of incredible momentum as the children of these young people take leadership roles at younger ages. Even with the 3% rule in effect—that only 3% on average will work consistently to achieve their goals—high achievers will establish a voice that cannot be ignored. I am part of that movement.

What made me tick was that I saw the system for what it was in relation to what I wanted to become. Institutions prepared me to

Let's Be Realistic

move into the job market, but they failed to teach me how to live abundantly. The staff, teachers, and supporters cared. In their minds, it was enough to conclude that a small percentage of these children would succeed. I would rather they thought that 100% of the children would excel. I would have been swept up into opportunity rather than limited to their low expectations. But ultimately, that is fine. My ambition and my achievement are up to me. Resources are limitless and should be extended to others who are at the bottom working to move up from where they are.

Application for You

Seek your way. I want everyone limited in their childhood to see a vision without limits. I know what it is like to be limited by health and resources. Leaders are visionaries.

Find people with amazing stories and match their energy. Recognize that education and support are the beginning. Business is the next step. Whether you work for someone or create your own entrepreneurial opportunity, you must run your work like it is a business. You must apply the information you have learned and expand on that information. Intentionally apply your lessons to build a legacy that lasts.

Darnelle Beckford

The ambition to make something for yourself must be insistent. I refused to allow society to tell me what I would become and the limit upon my life. Even when people told me that I could not, I went ahead and did it. You must tune out the limitations and persevere toward your goals with tunnel vision. People may have information on your file, but they don't know your story. Your story is your constant motivation to overcome. It is a reminder that you can overcome challenges because you have overcome issues in the past. It is also a consolation when you must try again because you know that your best life is yours to create. Let them be "realistic." Work to create your own reality.

When you ask what love is, you may be too frightened to see the answer. It may mean complete upheaval; you may discover that you do not love your wife or husband or children; you may have to shatter the house you have built. You may never go back to the temple or church.

JIDDU KRISHNAMURTI

Darnelle Beckford

About the Author

Darnelle Beckford is a Jamaican-American college graduate who completed his bachelor's degree in business management. Since the age of two, he has dealt with the social and developmental challenges associated with his neurological diagnosis. Mr. Beckford attributes his strength and the ability to stay positive and focused to the support and encouragement of close friends and family. Their support throughout the years helped him to surpass expectations and get through difficult times.

Mr. Beckford's journey was not an easy one. He encountered many struggles in life that defied belief. It takes determination, drive, and passion to beat the difficult odds that come along with life. Although there were difficult trials in his life, he had confidence in knowing that there is a light at the end of the tunnel. Beckford is proud of his dedicated Jamaican parents who strongly believe that

Let's Be Realistic

nothing is impossible. His parents had a strong belief that the path to success is education. He believes that the life God gave him has made him a stronger person. There is a traditional saying in Jamaica: "Hog say de first dutty wata mi ketch mi wash," which means "to make use of the first opportunity that comes your way". One of the many opportunities that he took advantage of was his education. Education and mentorship have become his focus. Support and encouragement for those young ones is critical to the success of society and what we all can achieve together.

You have reached the point where the victory is to be won from within what's and can only be lost from within.
Marcus Garvey

CPSIA information can be obtained
at www.ICGtesting.com
Printed in the USA
BVHW040242140721
611841BV00013B/1316